Young Adult's Financial Freedom Blueprint

Mastering Money for a Secure Future

(UK Edition)

HASSAN AFIFI

Copyright © 2023 Hassan Afifi

All rights reserved.

ISBN: 9798399947624

Reproduction or translation of any part of this work beyond that permitted by Section 107 or 108 of the 1976 United States Copyright Act without permission of the copyright owner is unlawful. Requests for permission or further information should be addressed to Hassan Afifi (books@hassan-afifi.com).

Please note the information contained within this document is for educational and entertainment purposes only. All effort has been executed to present accurate, up to date, and reliable, complete information. No warranties of any kind are declared or implied. Readers acknowledge that the authors are not engaging in the rendering of legal, financial, medical or professional advice. The content within this book has been derived from various sources. If legal advice or other expert assistance is required, the services of a competent professional person should be sought.

By reading this document, the reader agrees that under no circumstances is the author responsible for any losses, direct or indirect, which are incurred as a result of the use of information contained within this document, including, but not limited to, errors, omissions, or inaccuracies.

Hassan Afifi

Young Adult's Financial Freedom Blueprint –
Mastering Money for a Secure Future

CONTENTS

Introduction	v
CHAPTER I – Building a Strong Financial Foundation	1
CHAPTER II – Budgeting & Managing Money	7
CHAPTER III – Saving & Investing for Future Success	13
CHAPTER IV – Career Planning & Transitioning	25
CHAPTER V – Entrepreneurship & Financial Security	31
CHAPTER VI – Pensions & Planning for Retirement	37
CHAPTER VII – Emergency Savings & Financial Safety Nets	43
CHAPTER VIII – Practical Scenarios & Application	51
Conclusion	63
About The Author	66

INTRODUCTION

Close your eyes and imagine a world of endless possibilities unfolding before you. As you stand on the precipice of adulthood, there's an important secret to unlocking the door to your future success: mastering money. Welcome to "Young Adult's Financial Freedom Blueprint: Mastering Money for a Secure Future" – a guide designed exclusively for you, filled with exciting insights and practical tips to help you navigate the thrilling world of personal finance.

But hold on a second! Before we dive into this incredible journey together, let me share a bit about my own story. Just a while ago, I was in your shoes, eager to conquer the world and make my mark. I studied economics at university, and you know what really caught my attention? Business planning and investments! I couldn't get enough of it. So, I took the plunge and started investing even during my university days. But guess what? I made mistakes – loads of them! However, I didn't let those blunders discourage me. I turned them into valuable lessons that paved the way for my ongoing financial education.

Now, let's take a detour from the world of finance and plunge into an entirely different adventure. Picture this: I traded textbooks for a wetsuit and embarked on a thrilling career as a scuba diving instructor in the stunning depths of the Red Sea. Can you imagine the incredible experiences and stories that unfolded? And you know what else? I made some pretty decent money at the time. But here's the thing: I didn't pay much attention to my financial future back then. It was all about living in the moment and embracing the serenity of the underwater world. Little did I realise how crucial it is to secure our financial destiny early on.

Fast forward to the present. Life's whirlwind led me to the United Kingdom, where I found myself diving into the world of investments in a whole new way. The excitement and joy I once experienced underwater transformed into a passion for understanding the intricate dance of money, numbers, and financial planning. And that's why I'm here, writing this book, with one mission in mind – to share the knowledge and insights that I wish someone had shared with me when I was just about to embark on my own journey.

But hold on tight! Before we proceed any further, it's essential to clarify something. This book is not financial advice tailored specifically to your unique circumstances. Instead, it serves as an enlightening introduction to the world of personal finance. Think of it as your compass, guiding you toward financial independence. To navigate the treacherous waters of personal finance successfully, it's crucial to seek personalised advice from qualified professionals who can help you chart your own course.

Within the pages of this book, we're going to embark on a thrilling adventure together. We'll explore the secrets of budgeting, the art of money management, the magic of saving and investing, the thrill of career planning, the spirit of entrepreneurship, the mysteries of retirement planning, the importance of financial safety nets, and the comforts of proper passive income. But don't worry – we won't be talking in complicated jargon or snooze-inducing lectures. Instead, we'll share real-life stories, relatable examples, and exciting exercises to make the journey enjoyable and, dare I say, fun!

Remember, my story is just one of many, but it's my genuine hope that by sharing my experiences and the lessons I've learned, you'll find inspiration, guidance, and the tools you need to seize control of your financial future.

Are you ready to embark on this incredible adventure? Let's dive right into the first chapter, where we'll lay the foundation for building a solid financial future. Together, we'll unlock the secrets of financial freedom and set sail on the journey of a lifetime!

Young Adult's Financial Freedom Blueprint –
Mastering Money for a Secure Future

CHAPTER I
BUILDING A STRONG FINANCIAL FOUNDATION

In our journey towards financial freedom, we must lay a solid groundwork for success. Understanding the principles of financial literacy, cultivating a mindset of financial independence, and setting clear goals are crucial steps to shape our financial future. Additionally, we need to be aware of the dangers of succumbing to societal pressures, especially in the age of social media. Let's explore the key elements of building a strong financial foundation and debunk some misleading narratives.

Section 1.1: The Importance of Financial Literacy

Financial literacy serves as the key to unlocking the doors of financial independence. By acquiring knowledge and skills in personal finance, we empower ourselves to make informed decisions about money and navigate the complexities of the financial world.

Example: Consider the impact of financial literacy on student loans. Different credit reference agencies employ diverse scoring systems, resulting in variations in credit scores. Understanding your credit score and how it affects your ability to secure favourable loan terms is crucial. For instance, a good credit score can qualify you for a student loan with a lower interest rate, potentially saving you thousands of pounds over the loan's lifespan. On the other hand, a poor credit score may result in higher interest rates, making it more challenging to repay the loan.

Section 1.2: Cultivating a Mindset of Financial Independence

Financial independence goes beyond amassing wealth; it involves adopting a mindset that guides our financial decisions. By embracing principles such as delayed gratification, distinguishing between needs and wants, and developing disciplined money habits, we establish a solid foundation for a lifetime of financial success.

Example: Let's explore the concept of delayed gratification through an example. Imagine you want to purchase a high-end gaming console that costs £400. Instead of buying it immediately on credit, which would accrue interest, you choose to save for it. By setting aside £50 per month, you can achieve your goal in 8 months. This approach not only avoids unnecessary debt but also cultivates the habit of saving for future needs and goals.

Section 1.3: Setting Financial Goals and Creating a Plan

Setting clear financial goals and creating a well-defined plan are fundamental to achieving financial success. Goals provide direction and purpose, guiding our financial decisions and actions.

Example: Suppose your goal is to save £5,000 within two years for a study-abroad programme. Break down this goal into smaller milestones by calculating the amount you need to save each month. By setting aside approximately £209 per month, you ensure you stay on track and reach your goal within the desired timeframe. Having a specific plan empowers you to prioritise your spending, make conscious choices, and allocate funds that align with your goals.

Section 1.4: Introduction to Budgeting and Money Management

Budgeting serves as the foundation of effective financial management. It enables us to track our income and expenses, allocate funds to different categories, and live within our means.

Example: Let's consider a scenario where you are a student with a part-time job, earning £800 per month. Creating a budget allows you to allocate your income to cover essential expenses such as rent (£300), utilities (£50), groceries (£150), transportation (£100), and other necessary costs. With a budget in place, you gain visibility into your financial situation and ensure that your spending aligns with your income, avoiding unnecessary debt and financial stress.

Section 1.5: The Pitfalls of Showing Off and Succumbing to FOMO

In the age of social media, the pressure to show off and keep up with others can lead to financial pitfalls. It is essential to recognise the dangers of comparison, overcome the fear of missing out (FOMO), and prioritise our long-term financial well-being over superficial displays.

Example: Many social media influencers promote the idea of quitting education as a direct path to success. They often highlight famous entrepreneurs who dropped out of university, like Mark Zuckerberg and Bill Gates. However, it's important to consider the full context. These individuals were already from privileged backgrounds and dropped out of prestigious institutions like Harvard and Stanford. Their success stories do not represent the norm, and it is crucial to weigh the potential risks and benefits before making such a decision.

Conclusion:

Building a strong financial foundation requires understanding the importance of financial literacy, cultivating a mindset of financial independence, setting clear goals, and developing effective budgeting and money management skills. It is crucial to navigate the challenges posed by social media influences, remain cautious of false narratives, and make decisions based on sound financial principles. Remember, the path to financial freedom starts with building a solid financial foundation. In the next chapter, we will delve into the practical aspects of budgeting and money management, equipping you with strategies to make informed financial choices.

Young Adult's Financial Freedom Blueprint – Mastering Money for a Secure Future

Task 1: Setting Financial Goals

1. Take some time to reflect on your short-term and long-term financial aspirations. These can include saving for a specific purchase, paying off debt, or building an emergency fund.

2. Write down at least three financial goals, specifying the amount you need to achieve each goal and the timeframe within which you want to accomplish it.

3. Break down each goal into smaller milestones and identify the actions you need to take to reach them.

4. Create a visual representation of your goals using a vision board or a spreadsheet to track your progress.

CHAPTER II
BUDGETING & MANAGING MONEY

*I*magine having the power to control your money and make it work for you. That's exactly what budgeting and managing money effectively can do. In this chapter, we'll dive into the world of budgeting and explore practical strategies that will help you take charge of your finances. By creating a personalised budget, tracking your expenses and income, making informed spending choices, and implementing smart saving strategies, you'll gain the tools to navigate the financial landscape with confidence.

Section 2.1: Creating a Personalised Budget

Creating a personalised budget is like having a roadmap for your money. It helps you allocate your income to different categories, ensuring you meet your financial obligations while still having room for the things you enjoy. Let's break it down step by step.

Step 1: Identify your income. Calculate the money you earn from your job, part-time work, or any other sources.

Step 2: Track your expenses. Take note of your monthly bills, such as rent, utilities, transportation, and groceries. Include any other recurring expenses you have, like gym memberships or subscriptions.

Step 3: Allocate funds. Distribute your income across different categories, prioritising your essential expenses first. Consider setting aside money for savings and discretionary spending as well. This way, you can enjoy your money while still being responsible with it.

Example: Let's say you earn £500 per month from your part-time job. After deducting £100 for rent, £50 for utilities, £100 for groceries, and £50 for transportation, you have £200 left. You could allocate £50 for savings, £50 for entertainment, and £100 for discretionary spending. Remember, these numbers can be adjusted based on your individual circumstances and financial goals.

Section 2.2: Tracking Expenses and Income

Tracking your expenses and income is an essential habit that will give you a clear understanding of where your money is going. By keeping a record of your spending, you'll be able to identify areas where you can cut back and make more informed financial decisions.

Example: Let's say you've been spending money on eating out with friends. By tracking your expenses, you realise that you're spending an average of £80 per month on dining out. Being aware of this allows you to make conscious choices about your spending habits. Perhaps you decide to reduce eating out to once a week, saving around £40 per month. Tracking your expenses empowers you to take control of your money and make adjustments where necessary.

Section 2.3: Making Informed Spending Choices

It's important to differentiate between needs and wants when making spending decisions. By evaluating the value and long-term impact of your purchases, you can make choices that align with your financial goals.

Example: Let's say you're considering purchasing a new video game console for £300. Before making the purchase, ask yourself if it's something you truly need or if it's more of a want. Consider how often you'll use it and the potential enjoyment it will bring. If you're not a hardcore gamer and the console won't significantly contribute to your happiness, you may decide to allocate those funds towards a different goal, like saving for a trip or investing in a new skill.

Section 2.4: Strategies for Saving and Reducing Expenses

Saving money is a habit that can set you up for financial success. By adopting strategies to reduce your expenses and increase your savings, you'll be able to achieve your financial goals faster.

Example: Consider implementing cost-saving techniques in your everyday life. This could include meal planning to reduce food waste, buying items in bulk to save on groceries, or using public transportation instead of taking a taxi. Let's say you typically spend £40 per month on takeaway coffee. By brewing your coffee at home and bringing it with you, you can save around £20 per month. These small changes can add up over time and free up more money for your savings or other financial priorities.

Conclusion:

Budgeting and managing money effectively are key skills that will empower you to make informed financial decisions and achieve your goals. By creating a personalised budget, tracking your expenses and income, making conscious spending choices, and implementing strategies for saving and reducing expenses, you're taking important steps towards financial freedom. In the next chapter, we'll explore the power of saving and investing for future success, showing you how to grow your wealth over time. Remember, mastering budgeting and money management is a lifelong skill that will benefit you at every stage of your financial journey.

Task 2: Creating a Personalised Budget

1. Gather all your financial information, such as income statements, bank statements, bills, and receipts.

2. Categorise your expenses into fixed expenses (e.g., rent, utilities) and variable expenses (e.g., groceries, entertainment).

3. Analyse your spending habits and identify areas where you can reduce expenses.

4. Allocate a portion of your income towards savings and investments.

5. Use a budgeting app or spreadsheet to create a monthly budget that aligns with your financial goals.

6. Monitor your expenses regularly and make adjustments as needed.

CHAPTER III
SAVING & INVESTING FOR FUTURE SUCCESS

Financial success is not just about managing your day-to-day expenses but also planning for the future. In this chapter, we will explore the power of saving and investing early, understand different types of savings accounts and investment options available in the UK, and discover the benefits of compound growth. By developing a strong savings habit and navigating investments wisely, you can set yourself on the path to long-term financial security and success.

Section 3.1: The Power of Saving and Investing Early

Saving and investing at a young age can have a profound impact on your financial future. By starting early, you can take advantage of the power of compounding, where your money grows over time through reinvested earnings and interest. This means that even small amounts saved or invested early on can grow significantly over the long term.

Example: Let's compare two individuals, Emily and Sam, to illustrate the power of starting early. Emily starts saving £100 per month at the age of 25 and continues to do so until the age of 35, a total of 10 years. Sam, on the other hand, delays saving until the age of 35 and saves £100 per month until the age of 65, a total of 30 years. Assuming an average annual return of 7% on their investments, let's see how their savings grow.

After 10 years, Emily would have saved £12,000. However, thanks to the power of compounding, assuming an average annual return of 7%, Emily's savings would have grown to approximately £140,484 by the time he reaches 65. In contrast, Sam, who saved for 30 years a total of £36,000, would have accumulated almost £122,000. This example demonstrates the advantage of starting early and harnessing the power of compounding.

Section 3.2: Exploring Different Types of Savings Accounts and Investment Options

When it comes to saving and investing, there are various options to consider. In the UK, you have access to savings accounts, individual savings accounts (ISAs), self-invested personal pension (SIPP) accounts, and investment vehicles such as index funds and high dividend yield funds.

1. **Account Types:**

    - *Savings Accounts:* These are low-risk options offered by banks and building societies where you can deposit your money and earn interest. The interest rates vary but are typically lower compared to other investment options.

        For instance, a regular savings account might offer an annual interest rate of around 0.5%, meaning that if you deposit £1,000, you would earn £5 in interest over a year.

    - *ISAs:* Individual Savings Accounts (ISAs) are tax-efficient accounts that allow you to save or invest up to a certain amount each year without paying tax on the interest or investment gains. For the tax year 2023/2024, the ISA allowance is £20,000. ISAs offer various types, including cash ISAs and stocks and shares ISAs, providing flexibility based on your financial goals and risk appetite.

    - *Lifetime ISA (LISA):* The Lifetime ISA is a government-backed savings account designed specifically to help individuals save for two key life goals: purchasing their first home or saving for retirement. Opening a LISA can be a smart move for young adults who are eligible and have long-term financial goals in mind. Here's an example to illustrate the potential benefits of a LISA:

Example: Meet Sarah, a 25-year-old aspiring homeowner. She decides to open a Lifetime ISA to save for a deposit on her first home. With a LISA, she can contribute up to £4,000 per year, and the government provides a 25% bonus on her contributions, up to a maximum of £1,000 per year. This means that for every £4,000 she saves in her LISA, the government will contribute an additional £1,000.

Sarah plans to save £200 per month (£2,400 per year) in her LISA. At the end of the first year, her total contributions will amount to £2,400. With the 25% government bonus, her LISA balance will be £3,000. Assuming she continues saving at the same rate for the next four years, she will have contributed a total of £12,000 and received £3,000 in government bonuses.

After five years, Sarah decides she's ready to buy her first home. Her total savings in the LISA, including the government bonus, will amount to £15,000. This, combined with any interest or investment returns earned on the account, can be used as a deposit toward her home purchase.

By taking advantage of the LISA, Sarah not only benefited from her own savings efforts but also received a significant boost from the government bonus. This example highlights how the LISA can be an effective tool for young adults looking to save for their first home.

Remember, the LISA also offers the option to save for retirement, allowing individuals to contribute until the age of 50. The funds can be withdrawn tax-free after the age of 60, making it an attractive long-term savings vehicle.

Note: This example is for illustrative purposes only and does not account for any potential interest or investment returns, fees, or fluctuations in government policy. It's important to research the current rules and regulations surrounding the Lifetime ISA and consult with financial professionals to make informed decisions based on your unique circumstances.

- *SIPP Accounts:* Self-invested personal pension (SIPP) accounts are tax-efficient retirement savings accounts. They offer individuals greater control and flexibility over their pension investments. With a SIPP, you can choose from a wide range of investment options, including stocks, bonds, funds, and commercial property. Contributions to a SIPP receive tax relief, meaning the government tops up your contributions based on your income tax rate. It's important to note that a SIPP is primarily designed for retirement savings and should be considered as part of your long-term financial plan.

2. **Investment Types:**

- *Index Funds:* These are investment funds that track a specific market index, such as the S&P500 or the NASDAQ100. They offer diversification by investing in a broad range of stocks within the index. Index funds are often recommended for long-term investing as they provide exposure to the overall market and can deliver steady returns over time. During the growth phase of your investing journey, when you're focused on accumulating wealth, index funds can be a suitable choice. Past performance has shown that the S&P500 has averaged around 10-12% annual returns, while the NASDAQ100 has shown even higher returns, averaging around 14-16% annually (past performance doesn't guarantee future returns).

- *High Dividend Yield Funds:* These investment funds focus on stocks that pay high dividends. Dividends are a portion of a company's profits distributed to shareholders. High dividend yield funds can provide regular income through these dividend payments. They are particularly useful as you approach the point where you want to generate income from your investments. These funds can be considered as true sources of passive income, helping you sustain your financial needs over time. While the dividend yields can vary, on average, high dividend yield funds may generate dividend yields of around 4-8% annually, depending on the market conditions.

Section 3.3: Understanding Compound Growth and Building a Strong Savings Habit

Compound growth is a powerful concept that enables your investments to grow exponentially over time. By understanding compound growth and developing a strong savings habit, you can maximise the growth potential of your savings and investments. There are free online calculators that can help you determine savings targets and calculate compound growth. One such helpful resource is the savings goals calculator available on thecalculatorsite.com.

When investing for the long term, it's important to remember that market performance should not deter you, especially when you make regular contributions to your investment accounts. Instead of focusing on short-term market fluctuations, aim for average performance over a long period. By consistently contributing to your investments, you can benefit from dollar-cost averaging, where you buy more shares when prices are low and fewer shares when prices are high.

Example 1: Emily, a 25-year-old graduate, wants to save for a down payment on her first home. She sets a savings goal of £50,000 and plans to achieve it within 10 years. If she saves every month to reach this goal without receiving any returns on her money, she would have to put aside £417 every month. Assuming an estimated average annual returns on investments or interest on savings of 5%, she can use the "monthly payment calculator" on thecalculatorsite.com to determine the monthly savings needed to reach her target. After inputting the values, the calculator suggests that Emily should save approximately £322 per month. By consistently saving this amount and earning compound interest, she can achieve her goal of £50,000 in 10 years. Moreover, if she is investing the money in a LISA, she would actually need to put in £257.60 per month, since she would be getting the additional amount from the government to reach the monthly target of £322.

Example 2: James, a 30-year-old professional, wants to build a retirement nest egg. He plans to retire at the age of 65, giving him 35 years to save and invest. James sets a retirement savings target of £1,000,000. Using the savings goals calculator and assuming an estimated average annual investment returns of 7%, he discovers that he needs to save around £555 per month to reach his goal. If these contributions are made in a SIPP account, he would need to actually put in around £444 per month and still should reach his target. If he was not investing the money or putting it in a SIPP account, he would have had to save £2,381 every month to reach the same goal! By making regular contributions and harnessing the power of compound growth and making use of the right type of account, James can work towards a comfortable retirement.

These examples demonstrate how compound growth can significantly amplify your savings over time. By setting clear financial goals, using calculators to determine the required savings amounts, and consistently saving and investing, you can leverage the power of compound growth to achieve your financial objectives.

Section 3.4: Navigating Investments Wisely

When it comes to investing, it's crucial to approach it with caution and avoid falling for get-rich-quick schemes. Educate yourself about different investment options, assess their risks, and consider seeking advice from financial professionals.

It's important to note that investing in single stocks and cryptocurrencies can be extremely risky and volatile. It is generally advisable to consider them as investments on the side with spare money, rather than relying on them as the main source of long-term wealth creation.

By focusing on diversified investments, such as index funds, high dividend yield funds, and utilising tax-efficient accounts like ISAs and SIPPs, you can benefit from broad market exposure, tax relief, and reduce the risk associated with investing in individual stocks.

Conclusion:

Saving and investing for future success is a key component of financial independence. By starting early, exploring different savings accounts and investment options, understanding compound growth, and making informed decisions, you can build a strong foundation for your financial future. Remember, investing is a long-term endeavour, and it's important to balance risk and reward. By being proactive, staying informed, and taking advantage of the various accounts and investment options available, you can navigate the world of savings and investments with confidence and set yourself on a path to financial security and success.

Task 3: Setting up an Automated Savings Plan

1. Determine a specific percentage or amount of your income that you can comfortably save each month.

2. Open different savings and investment accounts specifically designated for long-term goals.

3. Set up an automatic transfer from your current account to your different accounts on a monthly basis.

4. Monitor your savings and investments progress regularly and increase the contribution amount whenever possible.

5. Explore different accounts and investment options available in the UK, considering factors like risk tolerance and time horizon.

Young Adult's Financial Freedom Blueprint –
Mastering Money for a Secure Future

CHAPTER IV
CAREER PLANNING & TRANSITIONING

Choosing a career path and navigating the job market can be both exciting and challenging. In this chapter, we will delve into the process of career planning and transitioning, from exploring career options to making informed decisions about education and employment. We will also discuss the importance of prioritising financial stability over social media-driven career expectations. By understanding your interests, evaluating your skills, and approaching your career with a strategic mindset, you can set yourself up for a successful and fulfilling professional journey.

Section 4.1: Exploring Career Options and Interests

One of the first steps in career planning is to explore different career options and identify your areas of interest. Take the time to research various industries, job roles, and potential career paths. Consider what excites you, aligns with your values, and matches your skills and strengths.

Example: Let's say you have an interest in technology and are curious about the field of cybersecurity. Start by researching cybersecurity careers, understanding the job responsibilities, required qualifications, and growth opportunities. Look for online resources, industry reports, and career exploration tools specific to the UK, such as government websites or reputable career websites. This exploration phase will help you gain insights into different career options and narrow down your choices.

Section 4.2: Evaluating Skills and Strengths

To make informed career decisions, it's essential to evaluate your skills and strengths. Identify the areas where you excel and the skills you enjoy utilising. This self-assessment will help you identify potential career paths where you can leverage your strengths and thrive.

Example: Consider taking online skills assessments or personality tests tailored to career exploration. These assessments can provide valuable insights into your strengths, weaknesses, and potential areas of growth. Additionally, reflect on past experiences, extracurricular activities, and part-time jobs to identify skills you have developed or areas where you have demonstrated proficiency.

Section 4.3: Making Informed Decisions about Education and Employment

Once you have explored career options and evaluated your skills, it's time to make informed decisions about your education and employment choices. Consider the educational requirements for your desired career path, such as university degrees, vocational training, or certifications. Evaluate the potential return on investment and consider the cost, time commitment, and market demand for the chosen educational path.

Example: Suppose you are interested in pursuing a career in graphic design. Research different educational options, such as graphic design degree programs or specialised courses. Evaluate factors such as the reputation of educational institutions, curriculum content, and opportunities for practical experience or internships. Compare the costs and potential career outcomes associated with each option to make an informed decision about your education.

Section 4.4: Navigating the Job Market and Building a Successful Career

Navigating the job market requires strategic planning and continuous skill development. Stay updated on industry trends, job market demands, and emerging opportunities. Polish your resume, develop your interview skills, and network with professionals in your desired field. Building a successful career often involves a combination of hard work, perseverance, and adaptability.

Example: Suppose you are interested in a career in marketing. Stay informed about the latest marketing strategies, technologies, and consumer behaviour trends. Join professional organisations, attend industry events or webinars, and connect with professionals through online platforms such as LinkedIn. Consider seeking internships or entry-level positions to gain practical experience and develop your professional network.

Section 4.5: Prioritising Financial Stability over Social Media-Driven Career Expectations

In the age of social media, it's easy to fall into the trap of comparing your career progress to the highlight reels of others. However, it's crucial to prioritise financial stability over social media-driven career expectations. Remember that everyone's journey is unique, and success should be defined on your terms, considering your goals, values, and financial well-being.

Example: Avoid getting caught up in the pressure to showcase extravagant career achievements solely for social media validation. Instead, focus on building a solid foundation for your financial future. Prioritise financial stability by setting realistic goals, managing your expenses, and making informed financial decisions. Remember that a successful career is not solely defined by flashy titles or material possessions but by overall satisfaction, growth, and financial security.

Conclusion:

Career planning and transitioning are important steps towards achieving financial independence. By exploring career options, evaluating your skills, making informed decisions about education and employment, navigating the job market strategically, and prioritising financial stability, you can set yourself on a path to a successful and fulfilling career. Remember that your career journey is unique, and it's essential to define success on your terms. Stay focused, embrace continuous learning, and remain adaptable as you pursue your professional aspirations.

Task 4: Exploring Career Options and Interests

1. Research different career paths and industries that align with your interests and strengths.

2. Make a list of potential careers that excite you and research the qualifications, skills, and education required for each.

3. Speak with professionals working in those fields to gain insights into the day-to-day responsibilities and job prospects.

4. Evaluate the financial stability and growth potential of each career option, considering factors like salary, demand, and long-term prospects.

5. Based on your findings, create a shortlist of potential career paths to explore further.

CHAPTER V
ENTREPRENEURSHIP & FINANCIAL SECURITY

Entrepreneurship can be an exciting and rewarding path to financial independence. In this chapter, we will explore the world of entrepreneurship and discuss ways to start a business while maintaining financial stability. We will also delve into the importance of balancing employment and entrepreneurial ventures, financial planning for business success, and setting realistic entrepreneurship goals. By approaching entrepreneurship with a practical mindset and avoiding the allure of flashy social media representations, you can build a solid foundation for financial security.

Section 5.1: Safe Ways to Start a Business while Maintaining Financial Stability

Starting a business is a significant endeavour that requires careful planning and financial stability. It's crucial to explore safe ways to embark on your entrepreneurial journey while minimising the risks associated with financial instability.

Example: Consider starting your business as a side project while maintaining a stable source of income from employment or part-time work. This approach allows you to test the waters, validate your business idea, and generate income while still having a financial safety net. By gradually transitioning into full-time entrepreneurship once your business gains traction and demonstrates sustainable growth, you can minimise the financial risks involved.

Section 5.2: Balancing Employment and Entrepreneurial Ventures

Balancing employment and entrepreneurship can provide a stable income stream while pursuing your entrepreneurial aspirations. It's important to find a harmonious balance that allows you to allocate time and resources effectively between your job and your business.

Example: Maintain open communication with your employer regarding your entrepreneurial pursuits. Ensure that you fulfil your work obligations and responsibilities while dedicating focused time and effort to your business during your personal hours. By managing your time efficiently and setting clear boundaries, you can navigate the demands of both employment and entrepreneurship without compromising your financial stability.

Section 5.3: Financial Planning for Business Success

Financial planning is a crucial aspect of building a successful business. It involves understanding the financial implications of your business decisions, managing cash flow effectively, and setting realistic financial goals.

Example: Create a comprehensive business plan that includes financial projections, expenses, and revenue forecasts. Set measurable financial goals, such as revenue targets, profitability margins, and return on investment. Regularly review your financial performance, track expenses, and make adjustments to ensure your business remains financially sustainable and on track for success.

Section 5.4: Realistic Entrepreneurship Goals without Falling for Flashy Social Media Representations

In today's social media-driven world, it's easy to be swayed by flashy representations of overnight success in entrepreneurship. However, it's essential to set realistic goals and stay grounded in your entrepreneurial journey.

Example: Rather than chasing instant success, focus on building a sustainable and scalable business. Set realistic milestones that align with your long-term vision and values. Emphasise the importance of continuous learning, perseverance, and resilience. Remember that true success in entrepreneurship takes time, dedication, and a strategic approach.

Conclusion:

Entrepreneurship offers a pathway to financial security and personal fulfilment. By starting a business while maintaining financial stability, balancing employment and entrepreneurship, practicing sound financial planning, and setting realistic goals, you can navigate the entrepreneurial landscape with confidence. Avoid being swayed by the allure of flashy social media representations and instead focus on building a business that aligns with your values and long-term aspirations. Embrace the journey, learn from challenges, and adapt as needed to create a sustainable and prosperous entrepreneurial venture.

Task 5: Assessing Business Ideas and Financial Viability

1. Brainstorm business ideas that align with your interests and skills.

2. Conduct market research to evaluate the demand for your product or service and analyse the competition.

3. Create a basic business plan that outlines your target market, pricing strategy, and financial projections.

4. Assess the financial viability of your business idea by estimating startup costs, projected revenue, and potential profitability.

5. Consider the financial risks associated with entrepreneurship and develop strategies to mitigate them, such as maintaining a financial safety net or starting your business as a side venture.

Young Adult's Financial Freedom Blueprint –
Mastering Money for a Secure Future

CHAPTER VI
PENSIONS & PLANNING FOR RETIREMENT

Planning for retirement is a crucial aspect of financial security, even for young adults. In this chapter, we will explore the importance of retirement planning, discuss different pension options available in the UK, including Self-Invested Personal Pensions (SIPPs), and provide strategies for maximising pension contributions and securing your long-term financial future. By understanding the significance of retirement planning and making informed decisions, you can take control of your financial destiny and enjoy a comfortable retirement.

Section 6.1: Understanding the Importance of Retirement Planning, Even for Young Adults

Retirement planning is not just about distant future concerns – it has a direct impact on your financial well-being throughout your life. By starting early, you give yourself the advantage of time and compound growth to build a substantial retirement fund.

Example: Let's consider two individuals, Sarah and James. Sarah starts saving for retirement at the age of 25, contributing £200 per month into a SIPP until she reaches 65, accumulating a total of £96,000 in contributions, in addition to tax reclaimed into the account. Assuming an average annual return on investments of 8%, Sarah's retirement fund could potentially grow to around £872,000.

On the other hand, James delays saving until the age of 35 and contributes the same amount until he reaches 65, resulting in a total of £72,000 in contributions and a potential retirement fund of approximately £372,000. That is half a million pounds less than Sarah! This example highlights the significant advantage of starting early and harnessing the power of compound growth.

Section 6.2: Exploring Different Pension Options in the UK, Including SIPPs

The UK offers various pension options, and one popular choice for self-directed retirement planning is the Self-Invested Personal Pension (SIPP). SIPPs provide individuals with greater control and flexibility over their retirement investments.

Example: With a SIPP, you have the freedom to choose from a wide range of investment options, including stocks, bonds, funds, and even commercial property. This allows you to tailor your investment portfolio according to your risk tolerance and financial goals. For instance, you could invest in index funds that track the performance of well-established indices like the FTSE100, or you may opt for funds that follow the performance of the S&P500 or the NASDAQ100 for international exposure. By diversifying your investments within a SIPP, you can potentially enhance your long-term returns.

Section 6.3: Maximising Pension Contributions and Taking Advantage of Employer Schemes

Maximising your pension contributions and leveraging employer schemes can significantly accelerate your retirement savings. Understanding the options available and making informed choices can make a substantial difference in building your pension fund.

Example: Many employers offer workplace pension schemes, where they match employee contributions up to a certain percentage. For instance, if your employer matches contributions up to 5% of your salary, contributing at least that percentage ensures you benefit from the full employer match. By taking advantage of this scheme, you effectively double your savings and fast-track the growth of your pension fund.

Section 6.4: Avoiding the Temptation to Prioritise Short-term Enjoyment over Long-term Financial Security

It's natural to face temptations to prioritise short-term pleasures over long-term financial security. However, it's crucial to maintain a balance and make decisions that align with your retirement goals.

Example: Consider the choice between taking an expensive vacation or increasing your monthly pension contributions. While the vacation might provide immediate gratification, boosting your pension contributions can significantly enhance your retirement nest egg. By using online retirement calculators, such as the ones available on "thecalculatorsite.com," you can determine how much you need to save each month to reach your desired retirement goals. This empowers you to make informed choices that prioritise long-term financial security.

Conclusion:

Planning for retirement is an essential step towards securing your financial future. By understanding the importance of retirement planning, exploring different pension options like SIPPs, maximising contributions through employer schemes, and resisting the allure of short-term pleasures, you can lay a solid foundation for a comfortable retirement. Remember, starting early and making informed decisions are key elements in achieving long-term financial security and enjoying the retirement lifestyle you desire.

Task 6: Assessing Retirement Savings Goals

1. Estimate your desired retirement income based on your current lifestyle and future financial needs.

2. Calculate the total amount needed in your retirement pot that would give you the desired income above (assuming investing in high dividend yield funds).

3. Calculate the number of years you have until retirement and consider the effects of inflation.

4. Use online retirement calculators or consult a financial advisor to determine how much you need to save each month to reach your retirement goal.

5. Explore different pension options available in the UK, such as workplace pensions and self-invested personal pensions (SIPPs), considering factors like fees, investment options, and employer contributions.

6. Regularly review and adjust your retirement savings plan as your circumstances and goals change.

CHAPTER VII
EMERGENCY SAVINGS & FINANCIAL SAFETY NETS

Life is full of unexpected events and financial setbacks. In this chapter, we will delve into the importance of emergency savings and creating a solid financial safety net. By understanding the significance of having an emergency fund, implementing strategies to build one, exploring insurance options, and overcoming the temptation to prioritise unnecessary luxuries over financial security, you can safeguard yourself from unexpected financial challenges and ensure peace of mind.

Section 7.1: The Importance of Emergency Savings

Having an emergency fund is crucial for handling unexpected expenses and financial emergencies. It serves as a safety net that protects you from falling into debt or derailing your financial progress.

Example: Consider the scenario where your car suddenly breaks down, requiring significant repairs. Without an emergency fund, you may be forced to rely on credit cards or loans, incurring high interest and potentially worsening your financial situation. However, if you have an emergency fund, you can cover the car repairs without incurring debt, ensuring financial stability.

Section 7.2: Strategies for Building an Emergency Fund

Building an emergency fund requires discipline and smart financial management. Implementing effective strategies can help you gradually save and grow your emergency fund.

Example: One popular strategy is the "pay yourself first" approach. This means setting aside a portion of your income for savings before allocating funds for expenses. For instance, you could aim to save 10% of your monthly income as an emergency fund. By automating this process, such as setting up a standing order from your paycheck to a separate savings account, you ensure consistent contributions towards your emergency fund.

Section 7.3: Understanding Insurance Options and Protection Against Financial Setbacks

When it comes to safeguarding your financial well-being, insurance plays a crucial role in providing protection against unexpected events and potential financial setbacks. While medical insurance is often the first type that comes to mind, there are other important insurance options to consider.

1. **Home Insurance:** Your home is likely one of your most significant investments, and protecting it from unforeseen events is essential. Home insurance can provide coverage for damages caused by natural disasters, accidents, theft, or other unfortunate incidents. It ensures that you have the financial support to repair or rebuild your home, protecting your investment and providing Contents Insurance: Alongside home insurance, it is equally important to consider contents insurance. This type of insurance covers the belongings within your home, such as furniture, electronics, appliances, and personal belongings. In the event of theft, fire, or damage, contents insurance helps replace or repair your possessions, allowing you to recover financially without the burden of significant out-of-pocket expenses.

2. **Car Insurance:** If you own a vehicle, car insurance is legally required in the UK. This insurance provides coverage in case of accidents, damages, or theft involving your car. It not only protects your vehicle but also provides financial protection against potential

liability for damages caused to other vehicles or individuals involved in an accident. Car insurance ensures that you can handle unexpected costs and legal obligations associated with driving.

3. **Travel Insurance:** Whether you're planning a domestic getaway or an international adventure, travel insurance is a valuable companion. It offers coverage for various situations, including trip cancellations, lost luggage, medical emergencies, or other unforeseen circumstances that may arise during your travels. Travel insurance provides financial protection, ensuring that unexpected events don't turn into financial nightmares.

4. **Income Protection Insurance:** Income protection insurance is designed to provide financial support in the event that you are unable to work due to illness, injury, or disability. It ensures that you continue to receive a portion of your income, enabling you to cover essential expenses and maintain your financial stability during challenging times. Income protection insurance is particularly valuable for individuals who are self-employed or do not have extensive employer-provided benefits.

While these are just a few examples of insurance options available, they highlight the importance of protecting yourself and your assets against potential risks. Each type of insurance serves a specific purpose and can offer valuable financial support when unexpected circumstances arise.

Remember, insurance is not an unnecessary expense but a wise investment in your financial security. Assess your needs, consider the risks you face, and explore insurance options that align with your circumstances. By having appropriate insurance coverage, you can mitigate potential financial hardships and ensure a more stable future.

Section 7.4: Overcoming the Urge to Spend on Unnecessary Luxuries While Neglecting Financial Safety Nets

It's essential to strike a balance between enjoying life's luxuries and prioritising your financial safety nets. Avoiding unnecessary spending and being mindful of your financial goals can help you maintain a strong financial foundation.

Example: Consider the allure of purchasing the latest gadget or going on lavish vacations while neglecting your emergency fund. While indulging in these luxuries may provide short-term satisfaction, it leaves you vulnerable to financial hardships in the face of unexpected expenses. By exercising restraint and prioritising the growth of your emergency fund, you ensure a solid financial safety net.

Conclusion:

Building emergency savings and creating financial safety nets are crucial components of financial well-being. By recognising the importance of an emergency fund, implementing strategies to save, exploring insurance options, and making prudent financial choices, you protect yourself from unexpected financial challenges and secure a more stable future. Remember, maintaining a balance between enjoying life's luxuries and prioritising financial security is key to long-term financial well-being.

Task 7: Building an Emergency Fund

1. Determine your target emergency fund amount based on your monthly expenses and comfort level. This should ideally be at least 3-6 months of your total monthly expenses.

2. Calculate how much you need to save each month to reach your emergency fund goal within a specific timeframe.

3. Set up a separate savings account specifically designated for emergency funds.

4. Automate regular contributions to your emergency fund by scheduling automatic transfers from your current account.

5. Resist the temptation to use your emergency fund for non-emergency expenses and prioritise rebuilding it if you need to dip into it.

Young Adult's Financial Freedom Blueprint –
Mastering Money for a Secure Future

CHAPTER VIII
PRACTICAL SCENARIOS &
APPLICATION

*I*n this final chapter, we will put our knowledge and understanding of personal finance into practice by exploring comprehensive practical scenarios. By applying the financial concepts we've learned throughout the book to real-life situations, we can develop the skills necessary to make informed financial decisions and navigate the complexities of the financial world. These practical exercises will empower you to solve financial scenarios while avoiding the influence of social media expectations, ensuring that your financial choices are based on sound principles rather than external pressures.

Section 8.1: Comprehensive Practical Scenarios

In this section, we will examine practical scenarios that incorporate elements from each chapter. These scenarios will cover various aspects of personal finance, allowing us to apply our knowledge and skills to realistic situations.

Example Scenario 1: Creating a Budget and Financial Goals

You have just graduated from university and landed your first job. You need to create a budget, set financial goals, explore investment options, evaluate insurance coverage, and make informed decisions about student loan repayment. Let's consider a specific example:

- Monthly income: £2,500

- Monthly expenses: £1,800

- Financial goals: Save £500 per month for retirement, £200 per month for a future down payment on a house, and allocate £100 per month for emergency savings.

With a monthly income of £2,500 and expenses of £1,800, we have a surplus of £700 per month to allocate towards our financial goals. Let's break down the goals:

1. Saving for retirement: In the UK, a common retirement savings option is a Personal Pension or Workplace Pension. Consider contributing to a pension scheme, which offers tax advantages such as tax relief on contributions and potential employer contributions. To reach the goal of £500 a month, one can put aside

£400 and get a tax relief of £100, bring the total contributions to the goal of £500 per month. Consult with a financial advisor or pension provider to determine the best approach for your retirement savings.

2. Saving for a future down payment on a house: Aspiring homeowners in the UK can take advantage of schemes such as the Lifetime ISA, which provides government bonuses on savings towards a first home. By putting aside £200 into a Lifetime ISA, the total contributions after the government bonus should be £250. Explore these options to maximise your savings for a future house purchase.

3. Emergency savings: Allocating £100 per month towards emergency savings is a prudent move. Consider opening an easy-access savings account with a UK bank or building society. Look for accounts that offer competitive interest rates and easy access to funds in case of emergencies.

By following this budget and allocating funds towards specific goals, you are taking proactive steps towards securing your financial future, preparing for homeownership, and building an emergency fund.

Example Scenario 2: Evaluating Major Purchase Decisions

Young Adult's Financial Freedom Blueprint –
Mastering Money for a Secure Future

You are considering purchasing your first car. Let's analyse a specific example:

- Car price: £15,000
- Financing options: 3-year loan with an interest rate of 4.5%
- Monthly budget: £2,000

When evaluating major purchase decisions like buying a car, consider the following:

1. Car price: The car price of £15,000 represents the total cost you will need to finance or pay upfront. Keep in mind additional costs such as Vehicle Excise Duty (road tax), insurance premiums, and ongoing maintenance expenses.

2. Financing options: A common financing option for car purchases is a hire purchase agreement. With a hire purchase agreement, you make fixed monthly payments over a specific term, typically three to five years. Consider the interest rate offered and calculate the monthly payment amount to ensure it fits comfortably within your budget.

3. Monthly budget: Assess your monthly budget by subtracting your monthly expenses, including rent/mortgage, utilities, groceries, and other necessary costs, from your income. This will help determine how much you can comfortably allocate towards car payments and associated expenses such as insurance and fuel.

When making a car purchase, it's important to evaluate the affordability of the monthly payments within your budget, considering the impact on your ability to save for other financial goals.

Section 8.2: Applying Financial Concepts to Real-Life Situations

Understanding personal finance is one thing, but being able to apply that knowledge to real-life situations is where true financial literacy shines. In this section, we will explore practical examples and case studies that require us to utilise our financial knowledge and problem-solving skills.

Example Scenario 1: Managing Debt and Student Loans

You have recently graduated from university with £25,000 in student loan debt. Let's consider a specific example:

- Interest rate on student loans: 5%

- Monthly income: £2,500

- Monthly expenses: £1,800

When managing student loan debt, consider the following strategies:

1. Choosing the right repayment plan: UK student loans are typically repaid through the income-contingent repayment plan. This means your repayments are based on your

income. Ensure that you understand the repayment thresholds and percentages associated with your specific loan type. It's also important to consider whether it makes financial sense to make additional voluntary payments towards your student loans or if it's more beneficial to allocate those funds towards other financial goals.

2. Making additional payments: If you have surplus income after meeting your monthly expenses, you may choose to make additional voluntary payments towards your student loans. This can help reduce the total interest paid over the life of the loan and expedite the repayment process. However, it's crucial to consider whether this aligns with your overall financial goals and if there are other higher-priority debts or savings goals to focus on.

3. Prioritising financial goals alongside debt repayment: While managing student loan debt, it's important to strike a balance between debt repayment and other financial goals. Assess your financial situation and priorities. For example, if you have high-interest consumer debt, it may be more beneficial to prioritise paying off that debt first before focusing on student loan repayment.

By analysing these strategies and considering your personal financial situation, you can make informed decisions on managing your student loan debt effectively while maintaining financial stability.

Example Scenario 2: Investment Portfolio Allocation

You have decided to start investing and are considering different asset allocation strategies. Let's examine a specific example:

- Total investment portfolio: £50,000
- Allocation strategy: 70% equities (index funds tracking S&P500 and NASDAQ100) and 30% bonds

When allocating your investment portfolio, consider the following:

1. Diversification: Diversifying your portfolio by investing in a mix of asset classes, such as equities and bonds, can help mitigate risk. By allocating 70% to equities and 30% to bonds, you strike a balance between potential growth (equities) and stability (bonds). Keep in mind that asset allocation should be based on your risk tolerance, investment goals, and time horizon.

2. Equity investments: Consider investing in US stock market index funds that track prominent indices such as the S&P500 or NASDAQ100. These funds provide exposure to a diversified basket of US-listed companies, offering

potential for long-term growth. Research and choose funds that align with your investment objectives and consider consulting with a financial advisor for personalised advice.

3. Bond investments: Allocate a portion of your portfolio to UK government bonds, also known as gilts. These bonds are considered relatively low-risk investments, providing stability and income through regular interest payments. Evaluate different maturities and yields to match your risk profile and income requirements.

Remember to regularly review and rebalance your portfolio based on changing market conditions and your investment objectives.

Section 8.3: Exercises to Solve Practical Financial Scenarios

In this section, we will engage in exercises specifically designed to solve practical financial scenarios. These exercises will challenge us to apply the principles of budgeting, saving, investing, and managing financial risks in a hands-on manner.

Example Exercise 1: Setting a Savings Goal

You have set a financial goal to save for a down payment on a house. Let's consider a specific example:

- Down payment goal: £50,000
- Timeframe: 5 years
- Expected annual return on savings: 6%

To determine how much you need to save each month to reach your goal, you can use an online savings calculator. Search for the "monthly payment calculator" on a website such as thecalculatorsite.com. Input the relevant details, including the desired timeframe, expected annual return on savings, and the amount you aim to save (£50,000).

The calculator will provide you with the monthly savings amount required to achieve your goal. It's important to review and adjust your savings plan periodically to ensure it remains realistic and aligned with your financial circumstances.

Correct answer: £716.64 per month (or £573.31 per month if deposited in a Lifetime ISA)

Example Exercise 2: Analysing Insurance Coverage

You need to evaluate your insurance coverage to ensure adequate protection against financial setbacks. Let's examine a specific example:

- Current insurance coverage: Car insurance with comprehensive coverage, health insurance with a high-deductible plan, and renter's insurance

To analyse your insurance coverage, consider the following:

1. Car insurance: Review your car insurance policy to ensure it provides comprehensive coverage that meets your needs. Evaluate the coverage limits, deductibles, and additional features such as breakdown assistance or legal coverage. Compare quotes from different insurers to ensure you have the most suitable and cost-effective policy.

2. Health insurance: If you have a high-deductible health insurance plan, assess whether it aligns with your healthcare needs and financial situation. Consider factors such as your average medical expenses, potential out-of-pocket costs, and the coverage provided. It may be beneficial to consult with an insurance advisor or explore alternative coverage options to ensure you have adequate protection.

3. Renter's insurance: Review your renter's insurance policy to verify that it adequately covers your belongings and provides liability coverage. Assess the policy limits, exclusions, and any additional coverage you may require based on your specific circumstances.

Regularly reassessing your insurance coverage and comparing options can help ensure that you have the appropriate level of protection while optimising costs.

Conclusion:

As we conclude our journey through the world of personal finance, it is vital to recognise the practical application of the concepts we have learned. By engaging in comprehensive practical scenarios, applying financial concepts to real-life situations, and solving exercises tailored to specific financial scenarios, we enhance our financial decision-making skills and develop a strong foundation for a prosperous financial future. Remember to rely on your knowledge and critical thinking skills while avoiding the influence of social media expectations, ensuring that your financial choices align with your goals and values.

Task 8: Applying Financial Concepts to Real-Life Situations

1. Create practical scenarios that incorporate elements from each chapter, such as budgeting, saving, investing, and career planning.

2. Analyse the scenarios and identify the financial concepts and strategies that are most applicable.

3. Develop action plans for each scenario, outlining the steps you would take to address the financial challenges or goals presented.

4. Implement your action plans and evaluate the outcomes, considering both financial and personal factors.

5. Reflect on the lessons learned from these practical exercises and apply them to future financial decision-making.

CONCLUSION

In "Young Adult's Financial Freedom Blueprint: Mastering Money for a Secure Future," we have explored the essential principles of financial literacy and laid the groundwork for your journey towards a secure and prosperous financial future. Throughout this book, we have emphasised the importance of understanding and managing your finances, avoiding the traps of social media-driven expectations, and making informed decisions that prioritise long-term financial stability over short-term indulgence.

As we conclude this book, let's reflect on the key concepts and takeaways that will empower you to take control of your financial life. We have learned the significance of building a strong financial foundation by setting goals, creating personalised budgets, and making mindful spending choices. Budgeting and managing money is not just about restricting yourself; it's about empowering yourself to align your spending with your values and long-term aspirations.

We have also explored the power of saving and investing for future success. By starting early and harnessing the benefits of compound growth, you can build wealth over time. We have discussed different savings accounts and investment options available in the UK, including the importance of investing in index funds and high-dividend yield funds at different stages of your financial journey.

In our exploration of career planning and transitioning, we have emphasised the need to make informed decisions about education and employment. By evaluating your skills, interests, and the financial stability and growth potential of different career paths, you can prioritise financial stability over social media-driven career expectations.

Entrepreneurship has also been a topic of discussion, highlighting the importance of safe ways to start a business while maintaining financial stability. We have emphasised the need for realistic entrepreneurship goals, avoiding the allure of flashy social media representations, and understanding the financial planning required for business success. For more detailed information on these topics, please refer to my other books on "Financial Freedom" and "Starting a Business."

The significance of retirement planning and pensions has been emphasised, urging young adults to consider the importance of long-term financial security. Exploring different pension options and maximising contributions can ensure a comfortable retirement. Remember, it is never too early to start planning for retirement.

Emergency savings and financial safety nets have been highlighted as crucial elements of a solid financial plan. We have discussed the importance of building an emergency fund, understanding insurance options, and resisting the urge to spend on unnecessary luxuries while neglecting financial safety nets.

As we conclude, I want to remind you that making saving and investing a habit is not a luxury but a necessity. Treat it as you would your bills or rent payments, prioritising it as an essential part of your financial responsibilities. By integrating saving and investing into your financial routine, you can achieve long-term financial freedom and security.

While this book has provided you with a solid foundation, it is important to note that it serves as an introduction and not personalised financial advice. Each individual's financial situation is unique, and seeking professional guidance is crucial for specific situations. To delve deeper into the topics we have discussed and explore other life stages, debt management, and more, please refer to my other books on "Financial Freedom" and "Avoiding Business Mistakes."

I encourage you to take action now and embark on your journey towards financial freedom. The knowledge and tools you have gained from this book will be your compass as you navigate the complex world of personal finance. Remember, financial freedom is within your reach, and by taking control of your finances, you can shape a future of abundance, security, and fulfilment.

ABOUT THE AUTHOR

Hassan Afifi is a UK-based investment professional. He started investing and trading in financial markets in the early 1990s while at university. He holds a BA in economics.

Hassan has worked in institutional equity sales, advising some of the world's largest fund managers on their investments across different geographies and sectors.

He has also worked in corporate finance, helping entrepreneurs start or grow their businesses, raise funds for their projects, and guide management teams through their financial planning processes.

Hassan returned to the investment world full-time in 2020 focusing on wealth management to try and help as many people as he can to achieve their financial freedom.

www.ingramcontent.com/pod-product-compliance
Lightning Source LLC
Chambersburg PA
CBHW070426240526

45472CB00020B/1390